Starting and Finishing Business Goals: The Importance of the Beginning and the End

In the world of business, goals are the bedrock of success. They provide direction, purpose, and a sense of accomplishment.

However, while many emphasize the meticulous planning and execution of every step in between, it's essential to recognize that starting and finishing goals often carry more weight than the how or the in-between parts.

This perspective shift can drive entrepreneurial success, offering a clearer, more focused path to achievement.

The Significance of Starting: Setting the Wheels in Motion

The Power of Initiation:

Starting a business goal is akin to the first spark in a combustion engine.

Without it, there's no movement, no progress, and ultimately, no success.

The initial phase of setting a goal is where ideas are born, where visions take shape, and where the foundation for future achievements is laid.

This stage is crucial because it represents commitment and intent.

It's the moment you move from thought to action, which is often the hardest part of any journey.

Overcoming the Fear of Failure:

One of the biggest barriers to starting is the fear of failure.

Many potential entrepreneurs are paralyzed by the thought of what could go wrong, rather than energized by the possibilities of what could go right.

By focusing on the importance of just starting, you can overcome this paralysis.

It's about taking that first step, however small, and allowing momentum to build.

Once the journey has begun, the path forward often becomes clearer.

Establishing Momentum:

Momentum is a powerful force in business. Once a goal is set in motion, it becomes easier to maintain progress.

This is akin to Newton's First Law of Motion: an object in motion stays in motion. The initial effort required to start a goal can lead to a cascade of actions that propel you forward.

This is why starting is so critical; it sets the stage for all subsequent actions and decisions.

The Journey: Navigating the In-Between

The Overemphasis on Process:

While the journey and the process of achieving a goal are important, they often receive disproportionate attention.

Business plans, strategies, and step-by-step guides can become so detailed and rigid that they stifle creativity and adaptability.

Focusing too much on the how can lead to analysis paralysis, where overthinking and over-planning prevent actual progress.

While planning is necessary, it's the flexibility and willingness to adapt that often determine success.

The Role of Flexibility:

In the real world, business goals rarely unfold exactly as planned.

Market conditions change, competitors emerge, and unforeseen challenges arise.

The key is to remain flexible and adaptable. Instead of being wedded to a rigid plan, successful entrepreneurs pivot and adjust their strategies as needed.

This adaptability is crucial, but it should always be aligned with the end goal.

The ability to navigate the in-between with a focus on the finish line ensures that you're not derailed by unexpected obstacles.

Learning and Growth:

The in-between phase is also where learning and growth occur.

Every challenge faced and every setback encountered is an opportunity to learn and improve.

This phase is rich with experiences that shape you as a business leader and refine your approach.

However, it's essential to keep these experiences in perspective.

They are means to an end, not the end itself.

The lessons learned during the journey should inform and enhance your ability to reach the ultimate goal.

The Importance of Finishing: Bringing Goals to Fruition

The Satisfaction of Completion:

There is immense satisfaction in completing a goal.

It's a tangible achievement that validates all the effort, time, and resources invested.

Finishing a goal provides a sense of closure and accomplishment that is unmatched by any other part of the process.

This sense of completion is crucial for motivation, as it fuels the desire to set and achieve new goals.

Measuring Success:

 Finishing a goal allows for the measurement of success.

 Without a clear endpoint, it's challenging to evaluate whether the efforts were worthwhile.

 The completion of a goal provides a benchmark against which future goals can be measured.

It offers insights into what worked, what didn't, and what can be improved.

This evaluation is essential for growth and continuous improvement in business.

Building a Track Record:

Successfully finishing business goals builds a track record of success.

This track record is invaluable for gaining trust and credibility with stakeholders, investors, and customers.

It demonstrates your ability to deliver on promises and achieve tangible results.

Each completed goal strengthens your reputation and positions you for greater opportunities in the future.

Psychological Impact:

The psychological impact of finishing goals cannot be overstated.

It boosts confidence, reinforces a positive mindset, and reduces stress.

Knowing that you can set, pursue, and achieve goals creates a cycle of positive reinforcement.

This confidence is critical for tackling more ambitious goals and taking on greater challenges in the business world.

Balancing the Start and the Finish

Setting Clear, Achievable Goals:

To effectively balance the importance of starting and finishing, it's essential to set clear, achievable goals.

Goals should be specific, measurable, attainable, relevant, and time-bound (SMART).

This clarity ensures that both the start and the finish are well-defined, providing a clear roadmap for the journey in between.

Prioritizing Goals:

Not all goals are created equal.

Prioritizing goals based on their impact and alignment with your long-term vision is crucial.

High-priority goals should receive the most attention and resources, ensuring that they are started and finished with the highest level of commitment.

By focusing on the most important goals, you can maximize the return on your efforts.

Celebrating Milestones:

While the ultimate finish is critical, celebrating milestones along the way is also important.

These intermediate achievements provide motivation and a sense of progress.

Recognizing and celebrating these milestones helps maintain momentum and keeps the team engaged and focused.

The End as a New Beginning

The Cycle of Continuous Improvement:

In business, the end of one goal often marks the beginning of another.

The process of starting and finishing goals creates a cycle of continuous improvement.

Each completed goal provides insights and lessons that inform the next set of goals.

This iterative process is the essence of business growth and innovation.

Reinventing and Evolving

Finishing a goal doesn't mean resting on your laurels.

The business landscape is constantly evolving, and so must your goals.

Use the completion of one goal as a springboard to set new, more ambitious targets.

This constant reinvention and evolution are what drive long-term success and sustainability in business.

Building a Legacy

Ultimately, the cycle of starting and finishing goals contributes to building a legacy.

Each goal achieved adds to the body of work that defines your business and its impact.

This legacy is what will be remembered and celebrated, making the importance of starting and finishing goals all the more significant.

Conclusion

In the realm of business, the emphasis on starting and finishing goals cannot be overstated.

While the journey and the how are important, they are means to an end.

The act of starting represents commitment and sets the stage for progress, while the act of finishing validates the effort and provides a sense of accomplishment.

By focusing on these critical endpoints, entrepreneurs can ensure that their efforts are directed towards meaningful, measurable success.

The journey in between, with all its challenges and learning opportunities, serves to support the ultimate goal: achieving and completing the vision set forth.

This perspective not only drives business success but also fosters continuous growth, adaptability, and innovation.

Please use the next few pages for your notes and debates.

www.ingramcontent.com/pod-product-compliance
Lightning Source LLC
Chambersburg PA
CBHW050248230526
45470CB00005B/2163